FOREIGN AFFAIRS STUDIES

ON THE WAY TO A NEW INTERNATIONAL MONETARY ORDER

Otmar Emminger

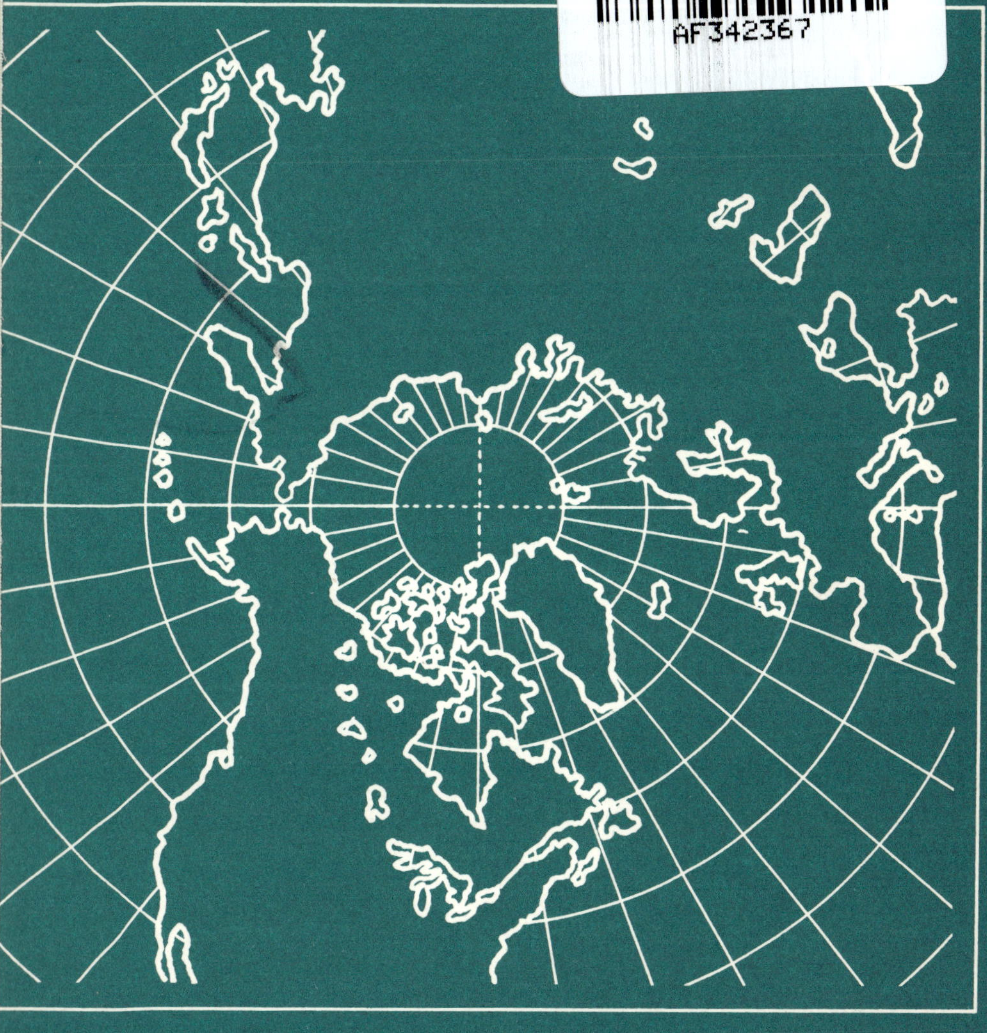

ON THE WAY TO A NEW INTERNATIONAL MONETARY ORDER

Otmar Emminger

American Enterprise Institute for Public Policy Research
Washington, D.C.

Otmar Emminger is vice-president of the Deutsche Bundesbank and deputy chairman of its central council.

ISBN 0-8447-3223-0

Foreign Affairs Study 39, August 1976

Library of Congress Catalog Card No. 76-40556

Printed in the United States of America

CONTENTS

ON THE WAY TO A NEW INTERNATIONAL MONETARY ORDER

Introduction

What the future international monetary order will look like is a question of topical interest, for we are just now in the process of clearing away the debris of the former monetary system—the Bretton Woods system of fixed par values—that broke down three years ago. At the monetary conference held in Jamaica in January 1976 important amendments to the Articles of Agreement of the International Monetary Fund (IMF) were agreed upon.[1] They were subsequently passed in due form by the Board of Governors of the IMF and will now be submitted to the parliaments of the member countries for ratification, presumably to enter into force in twelve to fifteen months' time. The most important of these amendments refer to the exchange rate system and to the role of gold and the special drawing right (SDR) in the international monetary system.

The formal enactment of the new IMF rules by itself will not very much change the monetary principles already being applied in practice. For the main part these rules will codify and make legal the practices that have evolved over the last few years. Since the introduction of flexible exchange rates, IMF members have been compelled to operate outside the former rules of the IMF agreement that are the

Address by Otmar Emminger, deputy governor of the Deutsche Bundesbank, before the Institute for Foreign Trade and Payments Law of the University of Würzburg; delivered on June 28, 1976, in German.
[1] On the meeting of the Interim Committee of the Board of Governors of the International Monetary Fund at Kingston, Jamaica, on January 7–8, 1976, see Edward M. Bernstein et al., *Reflections on Jamaica*, Essays in International Finance No. 115 (Princeton: International Finance Section, Department of Economics, Princeton University, April 1976), esp. Bernstein, "The New International Monetary System" (pp. 1–8), to which this essay is in part a response.

subject of the revision. What critics occasionally called "wild shoots" or "international monetary anarchy" will now be raised to the dignity of an officially recognized "monetary system."

The ambitious plans for comprehensive reform of the international monetary system, discussed in the Committee of Twenty of the IMF between 1972 and 1974, had to be shelved. Why? In the first place, because the most important reforms envisaged were based on, and designed for, a worldwide system of "stable but adjustable par values," but events since 1973 have postponed a return to a worldwide system of fixed par values to the far (if not inaccessible) future. Secondly, important parts of the general reform envisaged were overambitious from the very beginning and could not have been achieved even if circumstances had been more favorable than they were. As examples of overambition I would mention the consolidation of the so-called dollar overhang through a substitution account in the IMF, the elimination of the asymmetry of the former intervention system by means of a worldwide system of multi-currency intervention (along the lines of the European monetary "Snake"), and the strict rules for balance-of-payments adjustment on the basis of reserve indicators. In the event, these theoretical "blueprints" had to yield to harsh realities and particularly to the inevitable advent of flexible exchange rates.

1. The Collapse of Bretton Woods

Why did the Bretton Woods system of fixed par values collapse? Views diverge on this question, particularly between the two sides of the Atlantic. Many Europeans see the main reason for the collapse in the asymmetry of the former gold/dollar standard that allowed the United States to finance virtually any balance-of-payments deficit "painlessly" with its own currency and thus—through a balance-of-payments policy of "benign neglect"—to inundate the world with dollars. Many Americans, on the other hand, hold the view that the special role of the dollar as a universally used intervention and reserve currency did not permit the United States to adjust the par value of the dollar on its own initiative (for one thing because in their opinion most other currencies would have simply followed suit, and for another because a devaluation of the dollar would have been equivalent to a revaluation of gold and a loss in value of the dollar holdings of all other countries). In the opinion of these viewers the exchange rate policy of other countries, including the reluctance to revalue strong currencies like the Deutschemark and yen at the proper time, forced the inevitably "passive" dollar into an overvalued position.

According to the U.S. view, therefore, the Bretton Woods system broke down as early as August 1971 when President Nixon suspended the gold convertibility of the dollar in order to enforce a general readjustment of exchange rates vis-à-vis the dollar. It is true that the suspension of the gold convertibility of the dollar invalidated an important provision of the Bretton Woods agreement. But the core of the Bretton Woods system, namely fixed par values, did not definitely disappear, nor did the dollar cease to be used as a general intervention and reserve currency.[2] Par values for the major currencies were reestablished under the Smithsonian Agreement concluded in Washington in December 1971. On this occasion the American myth that the gold parity of the dollar could not be changed was given up under pressure from other countries. Moreover, as late as February 1973 the parity of the dollar was devalued by a further 10 percent in accordance with the rules of the former system.

In any event there can be no doubt that the system of fixed par values, and thus the Bretton Woods system itself, did not break down until March 1973. The last push was given by the huge dollar flows in February and March 1973, flows that created unmanageable problems of inflation in the recipient countries, mainly the Federal Republic of Germany. In Germany alone the foreign exchange inflows at that time reached the equivalent of about DM 24 billion within five weeks, inflating the German monetary system to an unbearable degree. Faced with a similar experience, Switzerland had already adopted a floating exchange rate in January 1973 in order to shield its monetary system against further inflationary inflows of funds. In March 1973 the Deutschemark, together with a number of other EEC currencies and two associated Scandinavian currencies, went over to a "joint float" in relation to the dollar and other currencies. It was already fairly obvious at that time that the world's leading currencies could not return to fixed par values in the foreseeable future. The IMF Committee of Twenty on Reform of the International Monetary System did not, however, yield to this view until a year later when worldwide chronic inflation and the oil crisis forced it on the IMF members.

The break-down of the fixed parity system was, however, not due to the dollar crisis of spring 1973 alone. Behind it lay chronic shortcomings of a more general nature:

(1) The system of fixed par values again and again led to inappropriate exchange rates because individual countries whose price and balance-of-payments movements diverged from the general trend of

---

[2] From August 1971 through March 1973 the rest of the world accumulated no less than 26 billion inconvertible dollars in their currency reserves.

the world economy were neither prepared to adjust their own demand and price developments to the existing exchange rate nor prepared to effect the necessary adjustment of their par value in good time. Adequate pressure for adjustment was clearly lacking in the system.

(2) The special position of the dollar as a universally used intervention and reserve currency—a special position which was not explicitly laid down in the Bretton Woods agreement but which formed part of its foundations—tied the system for better or worse to the strength or weakness of the dollar.

(3) The fact that the dollar remained overvalued for years not only resulted in massive confidence movements from the dollar into other currencies time and again but also distorted the structure of world trade and the world economy. A portion of the large investments of U.S. corporations in Europe, for example, probably resulted from inappropriate exchange rate relationships, just as the export structure of Germany and other countries was distorted by the incorrect exchange rate relationship to the dollar. I need only mention Volkswagen exports to North America as one example of this.

(4) In practice the regime of fixed par values gradually degenerated into a system of inflation in several ways: instead of fostering monetary discipline and internal stability in the deficit countries, it increasingly compelled the surplus countries to adjust to the higher level of inflation in the deficit countries.[3] This built-in inflationary bias was reinforced by the monetary asymmetry of the system: in the surplus countries the purchase of foreign exchange forced the central bank to expand the monetary base ("high-powered money"), whereas, owing to their accommodating monetary policy, the foreign exchange outflows did not lead to a corresponding contraction of the money stock in the deficit countries. Ultimately every imbalance leading to inflows of foreign exchange into surplus countries (even if based only on short-term capital movements) led to an increase in the global level of inflation.[4] It is therefore no accident that in the final years of the par value system, which were characterized by particularly large foreign exchange disequilibria as a result of capital movements, money inflation in Europe reached an unprecedented peak: in the three and a quarter years from the beginning of 1970 to March 1973 the money

---

[3] As early as 1964 the IMF pointed out that this had become the normal kind of adjustment. See International Monetary Fund, *Annual Report 1964* (Washington, D.C.: IMF, 1964), p. 28: "The result is that international adjustment through changes in relative costs and prices typically involves more upward adjustment in surplus countries than downward adjustment in deficit countries."

[4] A mere recycling of such inflows through national or international monetary agencies such as the IMF (as occasionally suggested by U.S. economists) would not undo the primary inflationary effect.

stock (in the wider definition of M_2) increased by no less than 54 percent in the European industrial countries, while in the main deficit country, the United States, the money stock (far from contracting) experienced an even faster expansion than before. The monetary system of fixed par values had become a "perfect inflation machine."[5]

The degeneration of the system was also reflected in the fact that, from the beginning of the 1970s, international liquidity—that is, the volume of international monetary reserves—rose precipitously, nearly doubling between the beginning of 1970 and the end of 1972, a period of only three years. The main reasons for this were the large balance-of-payments deficits incurred by the United States (and by a number of other deficit countries) and the creation of reserves through the international money markets (Euro-markets).

These shortcomings of the system resulted in an uninterrupted chain of international monetary crises with enormous speculation, closures of the foreign exchange markets, monetary inflation, and so on. Delayed adjustments of unrealistic par values, *dirigiste* controls (particularly on capital transactions), and general uncertainty in world trade characterized this decline of the Bretton Woods system.

2. The New Rules

What do the new rules hold in store for the international monetary order? By far the most important rules relate to the exchange rate regime. The former par value system will be abolished in due form. The members may—now de jure—freely choose their own exchange rate arrangements.[6] However, there is to be freedom of choice but not freedom of behavior: in their practical exchange rate policy members will be bound by a code of good behavior. First, they must collaborate with the Fund in order to promote general stability and maintain orderly conditions on the exchange markets; second, they must avoid manipulating exchange rates to gain an unfair competitive advantage or to prevent effective balance-of-payments adjustment. An aggressive exchange rate policy is thus forbidden.

A Return to the Par Value System? The revised Articles of Agreement expressly allow for the possibility that a uniform exchange rate regime—for instance, a general par value system—might be reintro-

---

[5] Karl Blessing (former president of the Deutsche Bundesbank), in a speech delivered in Munich on March 26, 1971, and published in Deutsche Bundesbank, *Auszüge aus Presseartikeln*, no. 27 (April 3, 1971). See p. 5 for quotation.
[6] Except that they may no longer peg their currencies to gold.

duced with a majority of 85 percent of the total voting power in the Fund. But even then participation would be on a voluntary basis for each member country.

However, the chances of a return to a general par value system are, for the time being, very slim if not nil, for two main reasons: first, inflation differentials between the industrial nations, and second, destabilizing money and capital flows which might assume intolerable proportions under fixed exchange rates. It goes without saying that it is impossible to maintain fixed exchange rates between countries whose inflation rates diverge as much as the inflation rates in the industrial countries have diverged in the recent past and as they still diverge: last year, for example, the rates of price increase in the large industrial countries ranged from 6 percent in Germany to 24 percent in the United Kingdom. It can be safely assumed for the future (as it was the case in the past) that in a number of industrial countries the government will not be able to bring price and cost inflation under firm and permanent control. Here there are involved the deep-seated differences in the social structures of the various countries and above all in their ability to cope with struggles for the distribution of income. In all likelihood disparities in prices and costs among major countries will emerge again and again, which in their external effects can only be coped with by flexible exchange rates.

Destabilizing money flows have of their own become a further source of disturbance. With fixed parities such disturbing movements are often provoked by the slightest uncertainty or by anticipation of later difficulties for a currency, even when there are no current major disparities in inflation rates. Moreover, political uncertainties, differences in interest rates, and other such factors may also lead to large movements of funds from one currency into another. The monetary unrest in the European fixed parity arrangement (the "Snake") in February/March 1976 has once more demonstrated how susceptible fixed par values are to such destabilizing capital movements. In this field new structural factors have emerged: the sharply increased share of foreign trade and payments in the overall monetary turnover of most countries and the increasing internationalization of money markets and banking and the huge volume of international liquidity have massively increased the capacity for disturbing money flows. Apart from a resort to *dirigiste* capital controls—of doubtful effectiveness, especially in the longer run—these destabilizing money movements can only be countered by greater flexibility in exchange rates, as the experience of recent years has shown.

There are also other factors that make a return to fixed par values difficult today. One is that, in the interest of greater steadiness in economic and monetary policy, more and more countries (like Germany and the United States in the last two years) are switching to control of monetary aggregates in accordance with preset targets. This makes monetary policy particularly sensitive to sudden money movements from abroad. The currency unrest within the "Snake" before the French franc's withdrawal in March 1976 (unrest which led to an inflow of money into the Federal Republic equivalent to DM 9.5 billion) has demonstrated that such monetary disturbances originating abroad can become a problem even if par values are fixed vis-à-vis only a few other currencies. Let it be said in passing that it would be an illusion to expect assured external equilibrium among countries that observe common or harmonized quantitative norms for their monetary aggregates, quite apart from the likelihood that only a few stability-oriented countries would be able to comply with such norms in the longer run.

Another factor to be kept in mind is that we would at present not even know how to establish a worldwide symmetrical intervention system—one without privileges for the dollar—and, in particular, how in such a system the intervention obligations and the settlement of balances by the United States should be determined. (The suggestion discussed in the Committee of Twenty to introduce a worldwide "multi-currency intervention system," which was taken up again by a leading French expert at the recent San Francisco International Banking Conference of June 1976, appears to me to have only illusory promise.[7])

Recent Experiences with Floating. The conclusion seems to be that for the foreseeable future we shall have to live with more flexible exchange rates. Our main task must be to make them work. I could dispense with going into the lively international discussion of recent years about the pros and cons of floating because, since that discussion began, even the opponents of floating have had to admit that under present conditions they are unable to offer a practicable alternative. I should, however, like to make a few remarks on recent experience with floating because they will allow some inferences on how floating will function in the future.

(1) On the positive side it deserves to be stressed that with the aid of newly flexible exchange rates the world economy has survived very serious disturbances since 1973—I mention here only the Middle East war, the oil price explosion, and double-digit inflation rates in

---

[7] André de Lattre (president of Crédit National), quoted in the *Wall Street Journal*, June 18, 1976.

7

many countries—without a major international currency crisis. The IMF itself, the custodian of the Bretton Woods system, summarized its views on this in its 1975 *Annual Report* as follows: "On the whole, exchange rate flexibility appears to have enabled the world economy to surmount a succession of disturbing events, and to accommodate divergent trends in costs and prices in national economies with less disruption of trade and payments than a system of par values would have been able to do."[8] It is indeed remarkable that even international capital transactions, for which gloomy forecasts had been made in the event of a transition to floating, have grown surprisingly in recent years. Moreover, after the transition to floating a number of major countries were able to lift *dirigiste* capital controls (such as, for example, capital export controls in the United States and capital import controls in the Federal Republic of Germany).

(2) Floating has helped to reduce a number of deep-seated distortions in the structure of international trade and payments—I mention here only the American deficit and the German and Japanese surplus positions. Of course, this was less the result of floating rates than of once-for-all shifts in the levels of exchange rates that had taken place to a large degree before the transition to widespread floating in March 1973 (in fact, mainly in December 1971 and February 1973). But in very general terms it can be said that floating has made it easier for countries to move away from unrealistic exchange rates and to approach "correct" exchange rates in a flexible manner. However, not all countries with large payments imbalances have in fact availed themselves fully of this possibility.

(3) For the Federal Republic of Germany and a few other stability-oriented countries (Switzerland, for example) it was of particular significance that the transition to floating ended the obligation to purchase dollars at a fixed price. Only in this way did Germany regain control over its own money supply. The transition to floating in the spring of 1973 marks exactly the point in time when the anti-inflation policy in Germany began to bite and when the German rate of price increase broke away from the general international inflation convoy. It is not an accident either that in the industrial countries taken as a whole the growth of the money stock decelerated noticeably from the middle of 1973.

(4) Floating thus gives the stability-conscious countries new freedom to pursue their anti-inflation policies. On the other hand, floating does not give deficit countries that are living beyond their

---

[8] International Monetary Fund, *Annual Report 1975* (Washington, D.C.: IMF, 1975), p. 33.

8

means carte blanche to continue living beyond their means. On the contrary, after a while it puts strong pressure on them to change their ways. For if such countries refuse to effect necessary adjustments in real terms—in real wages or in private or public consumption—the exchange rate for their currencies will continue to fall. Then the notorious vicious circle is set in motion: inflation, fall in the exchange rate, even more inflation through rising import prices, a further drop in the exchange rate, and so on. Floating does not permit inflation-ridden countries to escape adjustment: instead, home-made inflation is concentrated all the more on the country where it originates. The United Kingdom and Italy, for example, have had this experience in recent years.

The fact that in deficit countries floating exchange rates lead more easily to an inflationary vicious circle has led some observers to criticize floating as inflationary. In my view, it is more correct to say that floating makes it easier for stability-oriented countries to pursue a national stability policy, but more difficult for inflation-ridden countries to continue with their policies in the longer run. The pressure on an inflation-ridden country to contain inflation and achieve an adjustment in real terms—monetary and financial discipline—is probably stronger with flexible exchange rates than with fixed rates. Without the slump in the sterling rate it is unlikely that the wage restraint agreements between the British government and the trade unions would have come about. As to the general question whether floating fosters inflation, it should also be remembered that in a system of floating there is in all events much less external pressure to expand the monetary base in an inflationary way than in a system with compulsory intervention in the exchange markets.

(5) There are also, however, some clear deficiencies in floating. We have occasionally witnessed hectic fluctuations and overreactions, partly because of the time lag between exchange rate shifts and their effects on trade, partly in connection with confidence-induced capital movements. The most recent experience of the Swiss franc and the pound sterling are cases in point. It is obvious, however, that in these cases a system of fixed par values would not have been able to cope with the situation at all. Still, it remains true that completely free exchange rates do not always clear the market without disturbances and overshooting.[9] This has led to a call for management and control of foreign exchange movements by the monetary authorities.

---

[9] But compare the following statement in the most recent IMF *Annual Report:* "Floating among major currencies has been characterized by some reduction in the amplitude of exchange rate movements. These developments reflect in part the fact that disturbances in the global pattern of payments have been less

(6) It has sometimes been considered a negative feature of floating that countries have for a time escaped the adjustment function and the discipline of floating by raising large foreign exchange loans abroad, by massively supporting the exchange rate of their currencies, and—in a few cases—by restricting payments. In the period immediately following the oil price explosion, financing deficits instead of adjusting them through the exchange rate was often inevitable. For the rest, these experiences go to show how much some deficit countries feel—and fear—the pressure resulting from a falling exchange rate. The competitive depreciations that had originally been so much feared did not materialize. Instead there have been attempts to bolster exchange rates artificially through intervention on a massive scale.

A Mixed Exchange Rate System. How will the exchange rate system develop in the future? On the basis of experience up to now we can say that floating neither will be universal nor will it be completely free. In both respects we have a mixed system, and future developments are likely to continue along present lines.

Only a relatively small number of countries—sixteen in all—at present allow their currency to float vis-à-vis all other major currencies. But they include, besides the United States, such other major countries as Japan, the United Kingdom, France, Canada, Italy, and Switzerland. The countries whose currencies are floating in isolation account for as much as 51 percent of the total foreign trade of the IMF members. The second group of about a hundred (mainly smaller) countries peg their currencies either to the dollar or to another key currency, or orient themselves towards such composites as a unit of special drawing rights (SDRs) or of other baskets of currencies. In between there is, third, the small group of countries that have joined the European parity arrangement, the "Snake."

The "Snake" countries maintain fixed exchange rate relationships within a margin of ±2.25 percent vis-à-vis each other and float their currencies jointly as a currency bloc against the dollar and other currencies. France having withdrawn (for the second time) in mid-March 1976, the "Snake" today includes the Federal Republic of Germany, the three Benelux countries, and three Scandinavian countries, seven countries in all. Austria is not a member of the group but does in fact maintain a fairly stable relationship between its currency and the "Snake" currencies. The countries belonging to the "Snake" (excluding

---

severe than during the early period of floating rates; in part, however, they may also represent an improvement in the ability of the market mechanism and official policies to cope with the realities of a more flexible exchange rate system." (International Monetary Fund, *Annual Report 1976* [Washington, D. C.: IMF, 1976], chapter 2.)

Austria) account for about 23 percent of the total trade of IMF members.

There are good reasons for these differences in existing exchange rate systems, and there will probably be similar groupings in the future, although individual countries may switch from one group to another. It is interesting to note that the grouping whose exchange rate system initially gave rise to particularly high hopes for the future, the joint float of the "Snake" currencies, is subject to some doubts today. There are several reasons for this. The ambitious hopes that the regional fixed exchange rate arrangement of the EEC countries would form the stepping stone towards economic and monetary union by 1980 have been disappointed.

For one thing, the structural differences in the social and economic fabric of the EEC member countries have become quite apparent in the last few years and have torn the regional fixed rate arrangement apart. For another, the possibility of irrevocably fixed exchange rates as a vehicle for monetary union—an idea that appeared for the first time in 1962 in a proposal of the EEC Commission—has proved to be an illusion. For another, the idea that with respect to economic integration there are first and second rank members in the EEC (the rank depending on whether they belong to the parity club)—an idea which is still alive in the Tindemans report on European economic integration issued at the beginning of 1976[10]—has proved to be an obstacle to dealing realistically with the integration issue. In the monetary field, in any event, only a currency mini-bloc consisting of EEC members and nonmembers has remained, and it is burdened with the problems of fixed parities in the present period of inflation disparities. Nevertheless, this "mini-snake" still seems to offer sufficient advantages and attractions to the participants to justify its survival, provided that it does not itself become a source of monetary unrest and instability. It must always be remembered, however, that such a parity system will only be viable in the longer run if all members pursue harmonized economic, fiscal, and monetary policies on a common basis of stability. This is particularly relevant if the "Snake" arrangement should be extended again to those EEC states that are outside it at present. Should such a re-entry into the "Snake" be possible only with the help of massive mutual credit lines, instability and inflationary trends would probably be built into the system from the very start.

Some years ago much was said about the possibility that larger currency blocs might develop whose members would maintain fixed

---

[10] Leo Tindemans (prime minister of Belgium), *European Union*, supplement 1/1976 to *Bulletin of the European Communities* (Brussels: Commission of the European Communities, 1976).

parities vis-à-vis each other but would float their currencies jointly vis-à-vis other groups. There was some talk about a European currency bloc, a dollar bloc, and a yen bloc. These ideas have been pushed into the background by the actual developments of recent years because they would require exactly those parallel price and balance-of-payments trends of the respective members of the bloc that are today so conspicuously missing in the countries of Europe.

Today there is talk instead of a stability triangle or quadrangle of the "strong" currencies—the U.S. dollar, the Deutschemark, the yen, and the Swiss franc. At present the four "strong currency" countries do indeed demonstrate the convergence of relative internal stability and external strength that would be required for them to join together and maintain stable exchange rates among themselves. It is not a coincidence that the exchange rate of the U.S. dollar vis-à-vis the Deutschemark has been more stable in the year since August 1975 than it was for many years before. In this year it has moved within a margin of only about 5.5 percent (or ±2.75 percent around an imaginary middle rate). This stability in today's most important exchange rate relationship (implying at the same time a similar degree of stability between the dollar and the other "Snake" currencies) has proved to be a stabilizing element in the world economy in recent times when a number of other currencies were beset by considerable turbulences. And this has contributed to the fact that the European monetary unrest of the beginning of 1976 did not develop into an international monetary crisis.

The well-meant suggestions (which are mainly put forward by U.S. banking circles) that a zone of fixed exchange rates should be formally set up among these "strong" currencies are hardly realistic—not only because we know that the U.S. monetary authorities would at present not be willing to accept any commitment for an exchange rate peg of any type (and would not have the resources to defend it) but also because a certain flexibility appears to be imperative particularly in relation to the U.S. dollar. Destabilizing capital movements between the dollar and other currencies could, at the slightest disturbance, assume very large proportions.

3. After Rambouillet and Jamaica

The relative stability of the dollar/Deutschemark relationship since August 1975 underlines an important consideration which has been reflected in the revised Articles of Agreement of the IMF as in the agreement on the exchange rate system at the Rambouillet summit in November 1975: namely, that greater exchange rate stability cannot in the long run be enforced merely by intervention and exchange rate manipulation since the external stability of a currency must be underpinned by domestic stability. The Rambouillet communiqué states that exchange rate stability "involves efforts to restore greater stability in underlying economic and financial conditions,"[11] and similar wording was incorporated in the new Article IV of the IMF Articles of Agreement. There will no longer be an attempt, as in the Bretton Woods system, to impose stable exchange rates from outside by decreeing intervention points and international intervention obligations in the hope that internal economic and fiscal policies will follow suit. Instead, an attempt is to be made to achieve exchange rate stability from within by internal stability and with the help of market forces. This represents a sort of "Copernican revolution" in the approach to exchange rate policy.

We in Germany have always supported this approach. Basically, this was the core of the controversy between the (then so-called) monetarists and (then so-called) economists which arose within the EEC when plans were elaborated for economic and monetary union. The German representatives had then insisted that to demand irrevocably fixed exchange rates before first ensuring coordinated policies and durable economic stability in the participating countries would be tantamount to putting the cart before the horse—or to turning the economic community into an "inflation community" from the start.

The fact that exchange rate movements are intended in principle to follow fundamental market conditions does not, however, mean that intervention on the exchange markets by central banks can be entirely dispensed with. Today there is not a single country that practices completely free floating without any intervention by the monetary authority whatever. We live in a system of controlled or managed flexibility.

This is in part due to the experience already noted that foreign exchange markets left to themselves do not or cannot always ensure smooth balance. First, there are occasional hectic short-term fluctuations in exchange rates that have no real function and that are unnecessarily disturbing. Second, there are movements in the exchange rate in one direction—either up or down—that occasionally gather a momentum of their own and, through the bandwagon effect or through speculation, are exaggerated beyond an economically meaningful degree. Third, there may be extreme balance-of-payments situations, such as the situation after the oil price explosion where it was eco-

---

[11] "Joint Declaration at the Rambouillet Economic Summit" in *IMF Survey*, vol. 4, no. 22 (November 24, 1975), p. 350.

nomically impossible to achieve immediate balance vis-à-vis the oil-exporting countries through the exchange rate alone, so that massive exchange rate support, often with the aid of foreign exchange loans, was inevitable for some time.

Rambouillet and Managed Floating. A milestone in the development of controlled floating was the Rambouillet summit conference. There the major industrial countries unanimously agreed that "their monetary authorities will act to counter disorderly market conditions, or erratic fluctuations in exchange rates."[12] In order to ensure this the existing daily telephone consultations among the central banks of the most important countries were intensified, and in addition regular contacts were organized among the ministers and deputy ministers responsible for monetary matters in the major countries.

Even before Rambouillet similar principles for intervention in the exchange markets existed, but they had not captured the limelight. Thus, at the beginning of 1975, the central banks of the EEC countries had agreed on certain principles for intervention in the event of hectic fluctuations in the dollar. On a wider plane, following a proposal of the Committee of Twenty, the IMF had in the summer of 1974 established Guidelines for the Management of Floating Exchange Rates. These guidelines recommended that member countries (1) smooth out very short-run fluctuations in market rates, (2) offer a measure of resistance to market tendencies in the slightly longer run, particularly when they are leading to unduly rapid movements in the rate, and (3) if they so wished, develop a medium-term norm ("target zone") for their exchange rate and consult with the IMF on this norm. So far, however, no country with a floating exchange rate has given any indication of developing such a medium-term norm.

As early as from the beginning of 1974 the Deutsche Bundesbank's intervention policy on the foreign exchange market was guided by similar principles. In its *Annual Report* for 1974 the Bundesbank stated that in its intervention policy on the exchange market its guiding principle is that interventions should be made for the purpose of maintaining "orderly market conditions," but that fundamental trends in the market should not be counteracted.[13] However, not only have interventions served to maintain orderly markets from day to day: the attempt has also been made to moderate excessive fluctuations in the Deutschemark/dollar rate over extended periods of time.[14]

---

[12] Ibid.

[13] Deutsche Bundesbank, *Annual Report 1974* (Frankfort a.M.: the Bundesbank, 1974), p. 55ff.

[14] As concerns the result up to the present see ibid., *1975*, p. 50.

14

How can one decide whether exchange rate movements are merely "erratic fluctuations" or reflect "fundamental trends in the market"? Doubt is sometimes expressed, in part by central banks participating in these interventions, that such a distinction is possible.[15] In our experience in Germany, the difference in most cases can be found out in practice, although only after smoothing interventions have continued for some time, simply by the persistence and intensity of the movement. In any event the Bundesbank made large interventions over periods of many months in one direction or the other and yet was able to maintain its net foreign exchange position nearly balanced over the two years 1974 and 1975 (a slight net outflow of foreign exchange over this period being deemed quite desirable). This permits the conclusion to be drawn that on balance the Bundesbank did not intervene against "fundamental market trends."[16]

The call for smoothing interventions on the foreign exchange market, expressed at the Rambouillet summit, has often been misunderstood. Thus, it has been asked whether it would not have been in line with the Rambouillet agreement if something had been done against the steep declines in the exchange rates of the lira and sterling. But the Rambouillet agreement does not rule out even substantial exchange rate movements if they are due to underlying factors: on the contrary, it was recognized in Rambouillet that fundamental factors should work themselves out through exchange rates. A considerable part—no one can say with absolute certainty how much—of the downward movement in the exchange rates of these two currencies was undoubtedly due to fundamental factors. Furthermore, the participants in the Rambouillet conference had their eye primarily on smoothing out the fluctuations between the U.S. dollar on the one hand and the "Snake" and the yen on the other.

The recent international foreign exchange assistance for sterling in the form of short-term credit lines totalling $5.3 billion was, *inter alia,* justified by reference to the "spirit of Rambouillet"—that is, to help restore orderly conditions on the foreign exchange markets. This did not imply a judgment whether the present exchange rate for

---

[15] Thus, the Netherlands Bank in its *Annual Report* for 1975 recently pointed out that "attempting to make the distinction between erratic and fundamental fluctuations in market exchange rates and specifying that while the former should be redressed through intervention the latter should not . . . has proved illusory [and] . . . . has no real operational significance." (See Morgan Guaranty Trust Co., *World Financial Markets,* June 1976, p. 4.)

[16] A further proof that these were successful "smoothing" interventions can be seen in the fact that the intervention operations have yielded substantial profits to the Bundesbank, the dollars having mostly been bought while their value was on the low side and sold while their value was on the high side.

sterling is "appropriate" or "inappropriate": the large collective rescue operation is in reality mainly intended to give the British government a breathing space of a few months in order to effect the requisite fundamental adjustments in domestic economic policy—slowing down wage inflation and reducing the budget deficit—without being overly disturbed by self-reinforcing speculation against sterling. To the extent that the United Kingdom is unable to repay the loan out of its own resources by December 1976 it will have to fall back on its credit lines with the IMF. This ensures that if the government makes use of the loan assistance for an extended period of time it will have to accept the economic policy conditions of the IMF.

International Liquidity. Such cases, as well as the payments distortions triggered by the oil price explosion and the more extensive intervention on the foreign exchange markets, demonstrate that reserves and reserve credit still matter in a system of widespread floating. International liquidity and its control are still of significance. This problem was in the foreground of the reform discussion in the Committee of Twenty between 1972 and 1974. It remained unresolved, in part because of its inherent difficulty and in part because it proved to be too controversial.

It has often been doubted that the problem of international liquidity would still play a great role in a system of flexible exchange rates. It was assumed that in such a system most countries would adjust their balance of payments mainly through movements in the exchange rate, thus obviating the need to finance disequilibria with foreign exchange reserves or reserve credit. Besides, it was assumed that the United States would no longer play a great role as a source of uncontrolled reserve creation because under a system of floating no country is obliged to purchase dollars at a fixed price. Finally, in such a system, potential surplus countries could avoid the undesired inflationary effect of excessive international liquidity on their own monetary system simply by declining to make any net purchases of foreign exchange.

It is true that there have been some fundamental changes in all these directions as a result of the transition to a more flexible system. But we live in a mixed system in which not every balance-of-payments adjustment is entrusted to flexible exchange rates alone. There is not only foreign exchange intervention against short-term fluctuations—which should be offsetting over time, as was for instance the case with the foreign exchange operations of the Bundesbank in 1974 and 1975 —but for reasons already mentioned there is occasionally also longer-term intervention on the exchange markets on a major scale. And, finally, our mixed system comprises some important fixed parity areas on the one hand (the European "Snake"), and on the other the many countries that have pegged their exchange rate to a key currency. This has produced what the Bank for International Settlements recently has called "a bewildering combination of exchange rate fluctuations and large reserve movements."[17]

The problem of international liquidity thus continues to exist, although perhaps on a reduced scale. In recent years the U.S. balance-of-payments deficit has no longer been the main source of international reserve creation as it was in the final stages of the Bretton Woods system (although in 1974–75 there was still quite some voluntary accumulation of dollar reserves in the world). Instead, the international money markets, the Euro-markets, have moved into the foreground as a source of reserve credit. In the years 1974 and 1975 the balance-of-payments financing provided by the Euro-markets was several times higher than the reserve loans granted by official institutions such as the IMF, the EEC, and individual central banks. This creates special problems with respect to controlling international liquidity, which does not, after all, consist only of official monetary reserves.[18]

Is it really true that the need for international liquidity—that is, for currency reserves and reserve credit—is far smaller in a system of widespread floating than under fixed parities? The large amounts used for foreign exchange intervention in the first few years after the transition to floating seemed to contradict this assumption. Some experts thereupon promptly put forward the opposite thesis.[19] But this overlooks the fact that in 1974–75 special circumstances prevented really "free" floating—in particular the payments distortions resulting from the commodity boom and the oil crisis. Even apart from this, some deficit countries for a time deliberately maintained unrealistically high exchange rates, and this, of course, necessitated increased use of reserves or reserve credit. Both these experiences are not the results of free floating but rather of its opposite, the reluctance to accept (or even the impossibility of accepting) entirely free floating. One of the consequences of financing a large part of the sudden "oil deficits"

---

[17] Cf. Bank for International Settlements, *Forty-sixth Annual Report* (Basle: BIS, 1976), p. 136.

[18] Cf. Dr. H. J. Witteveen, managing director of the International Monetary Fund, in a speech of April 29, 1976, on "The IMF and the International Banking Community": "Enlargement of this role of private banks might well foster a climate of all-too-easy borrowing by deficit countries, thus facilitating inflationary financing and delaying the adoption of needed adjustment policies." (*IMF Survey*, vol. 5, no. 9 [May 10, 1976], p. 129.)

[19] Cf. John Williamson, "Exchange Rate Flexibility and Reserve Use," IMF Document (unpublished), 1974.

through reserve credits was the strong upsurge in world monetary reserves in 1974 (by a total of $36 billion); this was, so to speak, demand-determined and furnished proof of the great elasticity of the present international reserve system—in other words, of its adaptability to the demand for reserves.

Apart from special cases of this kind, it can hardly be disputed that as a result of floating the need for international liquidity for balance-of-payments purposes has diminished. This has also been confirmed by the IMF in its *Annual Report* for 1975 where it is stated that "the use of reserves, and the volume of reserves needed to support it, is smaller in circumstances of widespread managed floating than under the par value system."[20]

Even in a system of widespread floating, making international liquidity available in too elastic a manner, either through international and national monetary institutions or through the private credit markets, may weaken balance-of-payments discipline, facilitate the maintenance of unrealistic exchange rates, and intensify international inflationary tendencies. This is true even though in such a system an individual country can ward off undesired inflows of liquidity better than it can under a system of compulsory exchange intervention.

Concern about the appropriate level of international liquidity is therefore still justified even with floating. But better control of liquidity is not in sight. The solutions proposed up to now—for instance the proposal by the managing director of the IMF, Mr. Witteveen, to control the accumulation of monetary reserves by a sort of minimum reserve in the form of SDRs (special drawing rights), or the proposal to establish a substitution account in the IMF to convert existing foreign exchange reserves (and possibly gold) into centrally controllable balances with the IMF—hardly seem attainable. As the discussions in the Committee of Twenty have shown, many countries, including in particular the oil-exporting countries, are not inclined to accept any interference in their reserve management policy. Moreover, such proposals would hardly affect the provision of reserve credit by the international money markets.

Gold. In this connection I should like to say a few words on the role of gold. Gold is, after all, still a substantial part of official monetary reserves: even when valued at the former official gold price its share in total world monetary reserves of $228 billion amounted to as much as $41.6 billion at the end of 1975, while at a price of $125 per ounce (corresponding to the free market price in June 1976) official gold

---

[20] International Monetary Fund, *Annual Report 1975*, p. 38.

reserves would be worth about $120 billion. The monetary role of gold
is to be gradually reduced in line with the decisions made in Jamaica.
There will no longer be an official gold price. Part of the IMF's gold
will be sold successively on the markets or returned to the member
countries. Even though the mystique of gold is not yet dead, the future
fate of gold will probably be of only secondary importance for the
development of world trade and international payments. What in-
terests us in this general monetary context is principally the question
how far monetary authorities can still use gold in the future as an
international means of payment to cover payments deficits. At present
the answer to this is quite uncertain. We in Germany have tried to
contribute to a practicable solution by accepting gold as collateral for
balance-of-payments credits among central banks. As early as 1974,
when still under the rules of the former system, we used this method
in a well-known pilot case, the balance-of-payments credit of $2
billion from the Bundesbank to the Banca d'Italia. But this method
also has its quantitative limits.

Whilst gold is to be gradually phased out in its monetary role, the
special drawing rights (SDRs) artificially created by the IMF are, according to the communiqué of the Jamaica Conference (January 7–8,
1976), intended to become "the principal reserve asset in the international monetary system."[21] But whether they can really push the
present main reserve media—reserve currencies (the dollar and others)
and gold—into the background or even replace them is at present an
open question. Quantitatively speaking, they have been of minimal
importance up to now. Between 1970 and 1972 a total of 9.3 billion
units of SDRs (equivalent today to some $11 billion) were created—
which is an amount less than one-third of the amount of monetary
reserves newly created in the one single year of 1974 in the form of
foreign exchange. Under present circumstances, with the need for
reserves reduced as a result of floating and with the highly elastic
creation of reserves through the international money markets, the
creation of more special drawing rights could hardly be justified.

The quality of special drawing rights will be enhanced by the
new IMF Articles of Agreement. The possible uses of the SDRs have
been extended, and the interest paid on them has been recently ad-
justed to bring it somewhat closer to market rates, which could make
them more attractive. In addition, special drawing rights have gained
ground in recent years as an international unit of account not only in
transactions between monetary authorities and the IMF but also in the
commercial field. In quantitative terms, the special drawing rights will

---

[21] See *New York Times*, January 9, 1976, p. 1.

hardly achieve the central role that has, at least verbally, been assigned to them; but perhaps they will over time achieve a significant role as a neutral international unit of account.

The Role of the IMF. It remains for me to say a few words about the role of the IMF in the new monetary system.

Sometimes the opinion is voiced that the IMF has, so to speak, had the rug pulled from under its feet as a result of the abolition of IMF-controlled fixed parities. This is not quite correct. Even under the Bretton Woods system the influence of the IMF on the national exchange rate policy of its member countries was limited. The new IMF rules on the exchange rate regime may give the IMF a greater influence than in the years of "illegal" floating. The Fund is to exercise "firm surveillance" over members' policies and actions in the exchange rate field, in particular over the observance of the above-mentioned rules of cooperation and mutual consideration. How this mandate is going to be implemented in practice remains to be seen. I suppose there will be some strengthening of the guidelines for floating of 1974, and possibly an extension of guidelines to other exchange arrangements.

The most important role of the IMF, however, is in its influencing member countries' policies in connection with its balance-of-payments loans to deficit countries. Here I see a real resurgence in the importance of the IMF. It has been found that there is no other institution that can exert similar influence on the economic policies of member countries. Recently it has even been observed that international bank syndicates which grant balance-of-payments loans to deficit countries show increased interest in operating in tandem with payments assistance from the IMF and the economic adjustment programs that usually accompany it.

Criticism has been expressed that the IMF may have allowed itself to be pushed too far in the direction of granting assistance to developing countries, thus running the risk of becoming an aid agency and impairing its function as the custodian of monetary discipline in the world.[22] I believe that this danger is overrated. The fact that payments problems of developing countries account for a substantial portion of the IMF's activities is natural and not at variance with its original mandate. The decisive point is how this mandate is fulfilled— that is, whether the Fund is able to make reserve credit subject to appropriate conditionality and whether the total volume of such credit remains within tolerable limits. In both respects the Fund seems to have done reasonably well up to now.

---

[22] Cf. *The Economist*, January 17, 1976, p. 82: "Do we need an IMF?"

Conclusion

Does the new international monetary system represent real progress? Recently the secretary of the Treasury of the United States, Mr. William Simon, hailed the introduction of the new exchange rate system as "one of the most significant and beneficial international developments of the present decade."[23] I would prefer to label it the recognition of the realities of our time—the disparities in rates of inflation and in economic performance in general, the huge potential amounts of money that can easily be shifted from one currency to another, the erratic fluctuations in the gold price, and so on. We have learned a fundamental truth the hard way, that there can be no stability in the international monetary system except on the basis of domestic stability in all the major countries. In taking account of this fact, the new monetary system is more realistic than the old one and less crisis-prone. But it is not necessarily an ideal system. To paraphrase what Churchill once said of democracy: it is the worst possible system except for all those other systems that have been tried from time to time.

---

[23] Quoted in *New York Times*, May 31, 1976.

DATE DUE

Demco, Inc. 38-293

Cover and book design: Pat Taylor

RECENT STUDIES IN FOREIGN AFFAIRS

On the Way to a New International Monetary Order by Otmar Emminger reviews the world monetary situation after the collapse of the Bretton Woods system, the devaluation of the dollar, the Rambouillet economic summit conference, and the Jamaica conference of the IMF. The author foresees a long period of floating exchange rates, with the monetary world divided three ways—into the free-floating currencies, the currencies pegged to the free-floating currencies, and the currencies of the European "Snake." Neither a return to fixed par values nor a return to gold, he believes, is at all likely—but neither is an expanded role for special drawing rights.

Dr. Emminger views the present system as the beginning of a recognition that international monetary stability depends on domestic monetary stability in the leading countries, rather than as a great achievement in itself. Indeed, to paraphrase what Winston Churchill said of democracy, he concludes, "it is the worst possible system except for all those other systems that have been tried from time to time."

Otmar Emminger is vice-president of the Deutsche Bundesbank and deputy chairman of its central council.

$1.50

American Enterprise Institute for Public Policy Research
1150 Seventeenth Street, N.W., Washington, D.C. 20036